80041

60500
EDWARD THOMPSON

RW 11/12
NOV 72
TECH GW

Paul Atterbury's

WONDER BOOK OF TRAINS

D&C

David and Charles

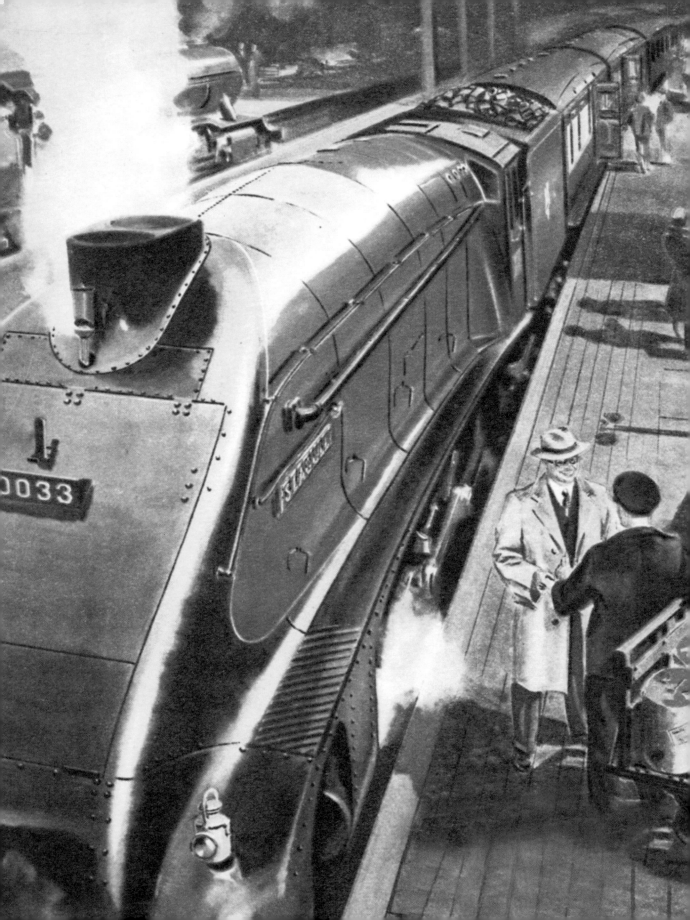

Paul Atterbury's
WONDER BOOK OF TRAINS

CONTENTS

INTRODUCTION

This book celebrates both the golden age of railways and the great days of railway picture books. The first half of the twentieth century witnessed a rich outpouring of exciting railway books, aimed mostly at young enthusiasts, and featuring colourful illustrations of railway scenes by a generation of artists whose work is now largely forgotten. In some cases, even their names have been lost. Unlike contemporary railway artists, whose work is usually retrospective or historical, these images, powerful, decorative, informative and technically accurate, represented the modern world of railways, in all its diversity, from Britain to the distant corners of Empire.

The many train books produced from the 1920s to the 1960s featured dramatic views of classic and modern locomotives, along with station and train scenes.

Also popular were views of the great locomotives built for the railways of the Empire, while later books feature diesel locomotives to illustrate the modern railway.

Early Railways

This 'coppernob' 0-4-0 locomotive, built for the Furness Railway in 1844, was a typical design of that era.

There have been railways of one kind or another operating in Britain at least since the 18th century, usually associated with mining and the transport of minerals.

These were primitive lines built over short distances, simply constructed with rails made from stone, timber or cast iron, and reliant upon horse or cable haulage.

Steam locomotives came into use during the first two decades of the 19th century. However, it is generally accepted that the modern railway age started in 1825, with the opening of the Stockton & Darlington Railway.

Another key date was the opening five years later of the line linking Liverpool and Manchester, an event preceded by the famous Rainhill trials, when George Stephenson's Rocket was not only triumphant but also established the principles of locomotive design that were to last over a century.

Many early railways concentrated on the transport of freight but the carriage of passengers became more important as the railway network spread rapidly during the 1830s and 1840s.

These three pictures show the early days of railways. Top, a locomotive takes on water at Park Side station on the Liverpool & Manchester Railway in the 1830s; centre, the famous Puffing Billy, built by William Hedley and Timothy Hackworth in 1813 for Wylam Colliery, and the world's oldest surviving steam locomotive; bottom, a print showing the celebrations that marked the opening of the Glasgow & Garnkirk Railway in 1831.

During this time many of the major trunk routes were either completed or being built, some radiating out from London, and others linking industrial cities in the north.

Over the same period there were important advances in the design and manufacture of locomotives and rolling stock, and gradual improvements in safety and performance, thanks largely to better signallling and train control.

A sequence of great railway engineers made their name in the planning and construction of the great trunk routes, with their massive cuttings, viaducts and tunnels that carried the lines across the many challenges presented by the diversity of the British landscape.

Two of the most famous were Robert Stephenson and Isambard Kingdom Brunel, brilliant men separated only by their differing attitudes to gauge.

Brunel used the 7-foot broad gauge for his Great Western Railway and its associated companies across the south and west of Britain, while Stephenson, and many others, were dedicated to the 4 foot 8½ inch gauge which, though narrower, was eventually to become the standard in Britain and many parts of Europe and the rest of the world.

By the 1860s the railway network had brought fast and efficient services to most of Britain's cities and towns, along with many of the country's more remote regions.

Stephenson's Rocket, dwarfed by an LMS 4-4-0 locomotive reveals
a century of progress and development.

One of the earliest named trains was the Great Western's Flying Dutchman, seen here running on Brunel's broad gauge.

• SIXTY YEARS' PROGRESS IN DESIGN AND CONSTRUCTION •

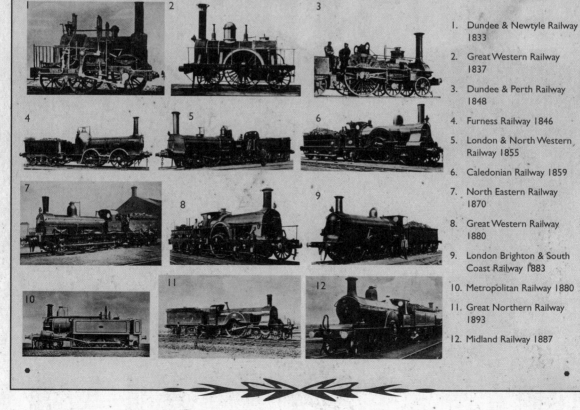

1. Dundee & Newtyle Railway 1833

2. Great Western Railway 1837

3. Dundee & Perth Railway 1848

4. Furness Railway 1846

5. London & North Western Railway 1855

6. Caledonian Railway 1859

7. North Eastern Railway 1870

8. Great Western Railway 1880

9. London Brighton & South Coast Railway 1883

10. Metropolitan Railway 1880

11. Great Northern Railway 1893

12. Midland Railway 1887

GREAT LOCOMOTIVES

There were numerous famous locomotives built during the Victorian era, but many of the classic types emerged in the 1920s and 1930s after the formation of the Big Four: the London, Midland and Scottish (LMS), the London and North Eastern (LNER), the Great Western (GWR) and the Southern Railways (SR).

This period represented in many ways the golden age of train travel in Britain, with modern expresses and high-speed goods trains operating all over the national network.

Each of the four regions produced memorable locomotive types, reflecting the extraordinary skills of a generation of famous mechanical engineers that included great names such as Gresley, Stanier, Collett and Maunsell. The quality of their work is underlined by the fact that most of their designs remained in use through the British Railways era and in many cases to the end of mainline steam in 1968.

While there were many regional and technical differences, caused by varying operational demands and attitudes to design, most of the classic locomotives of this era were Pacific types, with six driving wheels. In the late 1930s a fascination with streamlining and its impact on performance resulted in

With its streamlined shape and famous blue colour scheme the LMS's Coronation Scot was the most distinctive train of the 1930s.

By the 1950s the Southern Railway's Lord Nelson class of locomotives were not the most modern in the British Railways fleet but they were still earning their keep. Here, Sir Walter Raleigh, Southampton bound, is crossed by a modern electric train.

Another famous Southern Railway design was the Schools class.
This example, King's Canterbury, is leaving Charing Cross.

British Railway's Standard locomotives represented the final development of the steam engine in Britain. One was the Class 9 heavy freight locomotive, here hauling a mineral train out of the Severn tunnel.

A classic Great Western locomotive, Caerphilly Castle, heads an express bound for South Wales.

A Princess Royal Class locomotive at work in Cumbria.

An experimental gas turbine powered locomotive was used on BR's Western Region, in the search for modern train technology.

some notably elegant and modern-looking designs. The LNER's A4 class was the most famous, including Mallard, the world's fastest steam locomotive.

In the British Railways era from the late 1940s the challenge was to develop a mechanically advanced and standardised locomotive fleet, and this in turn produced some classic locomotive types for both passenger and heavy freight use.

At the same time, there were extensive experiments in Britain and many other parts of the world with other sources of power, including electricity, diesel and even gas turbine, to create the locomotives for the modern, post-steam, railway system.

From these came a series of successful classes of electric and diesel-electric locomotives, some of which are now considered classics in their own right.

The A4 Class Pacifics, designed by Sir Nigel Gresley and built by the LNER, included Mallard, the fastest steam locomotive in the world, seen here heading an Edinburgh express in the early days of British Railways.

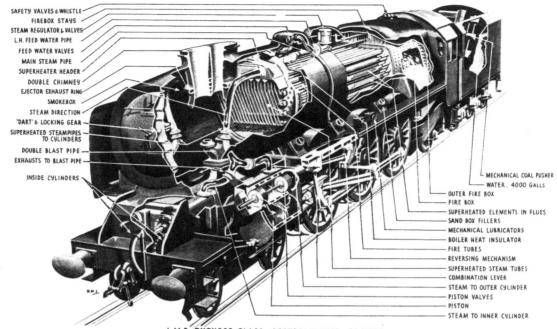

SAFETY VALVES & WHISTLE
FIREBOX STAYS
STEAM REGULATOR & VALVES
L.H. FEED WATER PIPE
FEED WATER VALVES
MAIN STEAM PIPE
SUPERHEATER HEADER
DOUBLE CHIMNEY
EJECTOR EXHAUST RING
SMOKEBOX
STEAM DIRECTION
'DART' & LOCKING GEAR
SUPERHEATED STEAMPIPES TO CYLINDERS
DOUBLE BLAST PIPE
EXHAUSTS TO BLAST PIPE
INSIDE CYLINDERS

MECHANICAL COAL PUSHER
WATER. 4000 GALLS.
OUTER FIRE BOX
FIRE BOX
SUPERHEATED ELEMENTS IN FLUES
SAND BOX FILLERS
MECHANICAL LUBRICATORS
BOILER HEAT INSULATOR
FIRE TUBES
REVERSING MECHANISM
SUPERHEATED STEAM TUBES
COMBINATION LEVER
STEAM TO OUTER CYLINDER
PISTON VALVES
PISTON
STEAM TO INNER CYLINDER

L.M.R. DUCHESS CLASS. DESTREAMLINED PACIFIC.

HOW IT W⚙RKS

A railway steam locomotive is a relatively simple piece of machinery whose basic principles of design, manufacture and operation were established by the 1850s, including such fundamental elements as the Walschaerts valve gear, though this great improvement to the basic Stephenson system was not widely used in Britain until the 1880s.

Subsequent developments have greatly enhanced the performance of the locomotive,

which is dependent upon regular and detailed maintenance, much of which has always been the responsibility of the footplate crew.

Driving a steam locomotive requires many skills, the key element of which is maintaining a constantly changing balance between fire and temperature, steam pressure and water supply, all of which can be affected by the weight of the train, the landscape and gradients, the state of the track, the quality of the coal and the weather.

Both experience and instinct are vital, particularly as every locomotive tended to be different in operation.

By comparison, the controls of a diesel or electric locomotive are more predictable and straightforward, the performance more consistent and the cab much more comfortable, though the mechanics are infinitely more complex and expensive to build. Early railway locomotives were famously varied and frequently eccentric but forms of standardisation were gradually applied to railways as a whole, including the international definition of wheel arrangements and the use of identifying head codes.

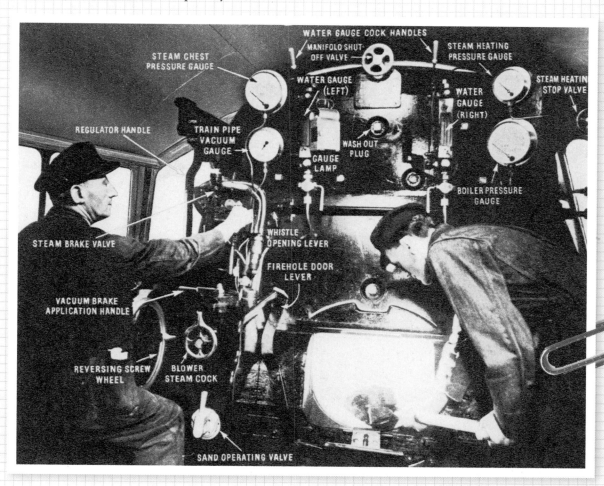

The layout of the controls in a modern British Railways Standard locomotive cab reflects decades of gradual development.

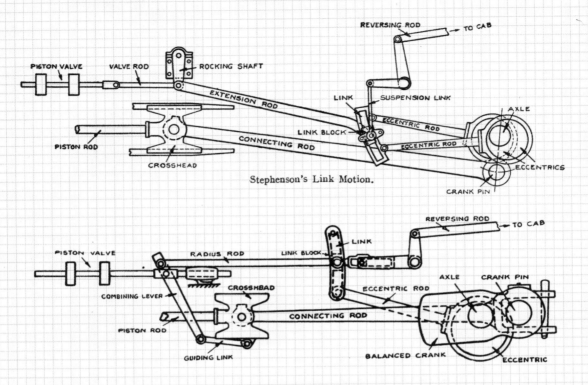

Stephenson's Link Motion.

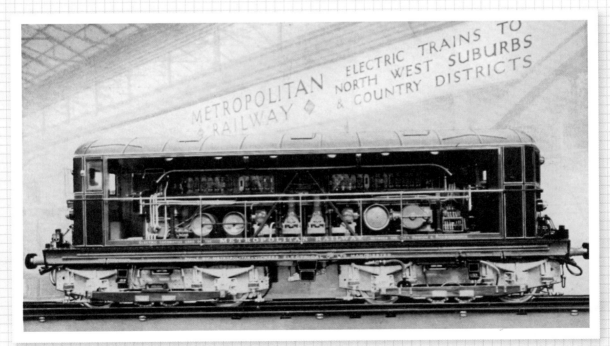

Stephenson's link motion and Walschaerts valve motion: the latter is the arrangement adopted by the Great Western Railway, though many other variants were used.

The mechanical complexity of an electric locomotive is revealed by this cutaway view of a famous Metropolitan Railway type.

LOCOMOTIVE WHEEL ARRANGEMENTS

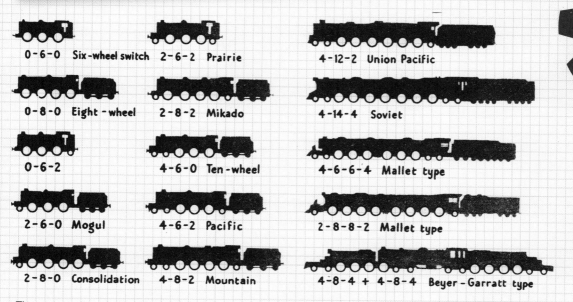

0-6-0 Six-wheel switch	2-6-2 Prairie	4-12-2 Union Pacific
0-8-0 Eight-wheel	2-8-2 Mikado	4-14-4 Soviet
0-6-2	4-6-0 Ten-wheel	4-6-6-4 Mallet type
2-6-0 Mogul	4-6-2 Pacific	2-8-8-2 Mallet type
2-8-0 Consolidation	4-8-2 Mountain	4-8-4 + 4-8-4 Beyer-Garratt type

There is an internationally recognised identification and name sequence for railway locomotives based on their wheel layouts.

Engine Headlamp Codes

In Britain, a standard system of headcodes was used to identify the type of train, i.e. passenger, express, goods, etc.

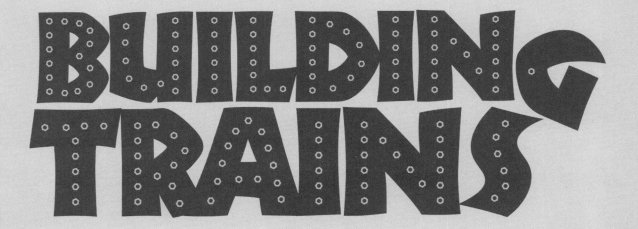

BUILDING TRAINS

By the 1850s large railway works dedicated to the building of locomotives had been established in many parts of Britain. The earliest were set up as independent operations and included some famous names such as Robert Stephenson, Hawthorn Leslie and the Vulcan Foundry, all destined for a long and successful life. However, better known were the works opened by many railway companies to build and maintain their own locomotives. Of which there were about thirty in England, Wales and Scotland.

A giant crane swings a new Royal Scot locomotive into position inside the LMS's Crewe Works.

Inch by inch the boiler and chassis of a new LNER A2 class
locomotive is married to its driving wheels at Doncaster works.

As the boiler is lowered onto the chassis, a new locomotive takes shape at the Great Western Railway's Swindon Works.

It is thought that by 1900 these works together were producing 2000 locomotives a year, including many built for export. There were also works dedicated to the manufacture and maintenance of carriages and goods wagons. Late 19th- and 20th- century mergers brought closures and rationalisation and, with the formation of the Big Four in 1923, SR, GWR, LMS and LNER, building work was concentrated at famous centres such as Swindon, Derby, Crewe, Doncaster and Eastleigh. With the coming of British Railways, there was further rationalisation but some of the surviving works were extensively rebuilt and equipped to produce a new generation of diesel and electric locomotives. At the same time, a specialised locomotive testing centre was established at Rugby. Main line steam locomotive building ceased in Britain in 1960, though some of the independent companies continued to build steam locomotives for industrial use and for export. In recent times, the specialised railway works have largely disappeared, and most of the great names have gone.

A newly completed locomotive is put through its paces on the testing rollers at Rugby Works.

ON THE FOOTPLATE

The driver of a steam train has always seemed a rather romantic but highly skilled figure, detached from the passengers in the heat and dust of the cab, with a job that was the ambition of generations of small boys. Yet, the reality of the job was far from romantic, with long hours spent in uncomfortable and often dangerous conditions. A steam locomotive is not a complex piece of machinery, but driving one successfully requires great skill.

It took years for a driver to be trained and qualified, having started as a cleaner and then progressed to fireman. Every locomotive is always a challenge to the combined skills of the driver and fireman. In social terms the engine driver was traditionally a well-respected figure, not far below the station master in the railway hierarchy.

The driver of a steam locomotive was a highly respected and very skilled man, with years of experience based on time spent first as a cleaner and then as a fireman. In this classic scene the driver waits, with his hand on the brake, for the signal to give him the road.

The Golden Arrow, one of the most famous of all named trains, is ready to depart from London's Victoria station.

TRAINS WITH NAMES

The Irish Mail, which dates back to 1848, was Britain's first officially named, or titled, train. There were other early contenders, such as the Flying Dutchman, named after a race horse, or the Zulu, named after the Zulu wars, but these were unofficial names used by railwaymen. Even the famous Flying Scotsman started as an unofficial name in the 1870s, not becoming an official titled train until 1923.

Names began to be used regularly from the 1880s, but these were usually functional rather than descriptive, such as the Pullman Limited Express. Indeed, the spread of Pullmans encouraged a spate of naming, as did the Club trains that were popular in the 1890s.

The Great Western's famous Cornish Riviera Express started running in the Edwardian era, as did the less familiar Sunny South Special, which connected Liverpool and Manchester with Brighton, in many ways a forerunner of the better known Pines Express, which carried generations of holiday-makers between industrial towns in the north-west and south coast resorts such as Bournemouth.

Naming remained rather an ad hoc process until the 1920s, when the Big Four began to take it more seriously, usually for competitive reasons. Thus, the Southern launched the Atlantic Coast Express in 1926 to compete against the Great Western's Cornish Riviera Express.

With a streamlined A4 in charge, the Capitals Limited starts its journey to Edinburgh.

The Flying Scotsman sets off from King's Cross for Edinburgh.

Surrounded by smoke and steam, The Great Western's Pembroke Coast Express races out of a tunnel en route to South Wales.

The Red Dragon races through a station in rural Wales.

The Broadsman crosses East Anglia towards Norwich.

Similarly, a number of competing trains appeared on the London to Scotland routes, following the Flying Scotsman's lead. These included the Royal Scot, the Mid Day Scot, the Thames-Clyde Express and a number of others. In the 1930s the battle continued, with the LNER's Silver Jubilee and Coronation, and the LMS's response with the Coronation Scot. Other famous names to emerge at this time were the Golden Arrow, the famous all-Pullman boat train between London and Dover, and the Great Western's Cheltenham Spa Express, more familiar as the Cheltenham Flyer and advertised for a while as the fastest train in the world. Others of this era include the Eastern Belle, running to Clacton, the Cambrian Coast Express, the Lancastrian and the Peaks Express. Another 1930s innovation was the Night Ferry, the rather prosaic name for the direct overnight train ferry service linking London with Paris and Brussels.

With the formation of British Railways, naming initially came to a halt, and then returned with a will on services all over Britain during the 1950s.

Names were quite diverse, with some linked to the route or the destination, while others were more imaginative or historical. Among the former were the North Briton, the Midland Pullman, the Broadsman, the Fenman, the Northumbrian, the Hook Continental, the Pembroke Coast Express and the series of Southern Belles – Devon, Bournemouth, Brighton, Kentish and Thanet.

The latter included the Robin Hood, the Red Dragon, the Merchant Venturer, the Bon Accord, the Easterling, the Clansman, the Cathedrals Express and the Fair Maid, later renamed the Morning Talisman. Some were quite short-lived, while others remained in the timetables for years, in one form or another.

Throughout this long period, the names were generally regarded with pride, and the locomotives usually carried a headboard proclaiming the title. Some were the subject of particular advertising, and considerable passenger loyalty was generated. Many names were dropped in the 1970s and 1980s, considered no longer relevant in the modern business world of British Rail and Intercity. Similar attitudes were behind the introduction of a series of trains with the word Executive in their titles, but they soon disappeared.

Since then, the naming of trains has been more erratic, with some railway operating companies keen to maintain the tradition and introduce names, while others have shown little interest. GNER, for example, made much of the Flying Scotsman name, and other recent introductions include the Wessex Scot and the Dorset Scot, the South Yorkshireman, the Highland Chieftain, the Golden Hind, the Caledonian Sleeper and the Virgin Invader.

The Devon Belle features a Pullman observation car.

The Brighton Belle, the famous electric Pullman train.

A Royal Scot locomotive hauls the Irish Mail across the Britannia Bridge over the Menai Straits.

The all-Pullman Southern Belle was a steam-hauled predecessor of the Brighton Belle.

The Cornish Riviera Express, seen here at Dawlish in Devon, is the Great Western's most famous named train.

A Southern Region Battle of Britain Class locomotive approaches journey's end with the all-Pullman Thanet Belle.

A British Railway Standard Class 7 locomotive waits to take the Norfolkman out of Liverpool Street station.

Two diesel electric locomotives haul the southbound Royal Scot out of Shugborough tunnel in Staffordshire.

The Yorkshire Pullman speeds northwards through London's home counties, running non-stop to Doncaster.

Sadly, locomotive headboards have been replaced largely by paper window stickers, and the process has become more ephemeral.

Less understandable perhaps is the use of American names, such as the 21st Century Limited and the Zephyr, for Grand Central's services between London and the north-east.

Overall, named trains have greatly enriched railway history and the railway landscape as a whole.

Some named trains have become internationally famous and featured in films and books, while others were short-lived and quickly forgotten.

Since the start of the naming process in the 1840s, well over 120 trains in Britain have carried official names that were listed in the timetable. There are many others with unofficial names that never made it into the timetable.

The guard watched the collection of the mail sacks from the lineside, triggered by the speeding train.

THE MAIL TRAIN

When the Liverpool & Manchester Railway opened in 1830, the Superintendent of Mail Coaches approached the Board and asked if their trains could carry the mail. Soon, two trains per day each way were earning revenue by carrying mail between the two cities.

Following this start, the carriage of the mail by train spread rapidly, a process regularised by an 1838 Act of Parliament that gave the Post Master General the right to insist on the mail being carried by any train, in carriages dedicated to that purpose. The Act also brought into being the Travelling Post Office, in which letters could be sorted and franked en route.

By the 1850s various companies began to operate special mail trains, running to set timetables and linking a series of distribution points at major stations and depots around Britain.

In the 1880s carriages that carried sorting staff were fitted with post boxes, enabling members of the public to post letters directly into the mail trains.

As the service expanded, the manual loading and unloading of sacks of mail began to delay the trains, and so a technique was developed from the 1840s for the mechanical exchange of mail bags between a moving train and trackside exchange equipment.

This featured machinery on the train to detach and catch with a net mailbags hanging from a column by the track, and to drop bags that would be caught by a trackside device.

At the peak of the service, shortly before World War 1, there were nearly 250 places where mail bag exchanges with a moving train could take place but from this point there was a steady decline, largely due to the increased use of motor vehicles by the General Post Office (GPO). The last exchange on the mainline network was in 1971.

The Travelling Post Office lived on, with the internal design of the carriages established in the early days.

On one side of the carriage were pigeon holes or racks for letter sorting, on the other storage space for mail sacks and tables where the staff worked.

The exchange device, if fitted, was only on one side, and so mail carriages sometimes had to be turned round between journeys.

While the sorters carry on with their tasks, the carriage doors have been opened and the net extended to catch the approaching mail bag. Meanwhile, lower down another bag is ready to be caught by the exchange device.

In this Travelling Post Office scene, postal workers are sorting the mail as the train races through the night. Spare sacks hang ready on the left.

The layout of a Travelling Post Office remained unchanged from the 1850s, with the sorters' pigeon holes on one side and the doors on the other.

This famous painting by Sir William Orpen, entitled The Night Mail, was owned by the London, Midland & Scottish Railway.

Postmen of the British Empire was a postcard series published in 1904. In this picture, the Night Mail is preparing to depart and postmen in their red uniforms are loading mail sacks into the guard's van.

Gangways, usually to one side, and connections between carriages, were normal, to enable the postal staff to move around freely.

In 1883 the railways began to carry parcels and by the early 1920s the GPO was sending 90 per cent of its parcels by rail, often in dedicated parcels trains running, like the mail trains, to nationwide schedules. Some parcel sorting was carried out on the trains but there was no real parcels equivalent of the Travelling Post Office. Mobile post offices, with telegraph, telephone and postal services, were introduced for a while from 1936.

From the 1960s train-based postal services were increasingly affected by road and air transport and so the network was steadily reduced. The railways responded by introducing a more efficient network with new distribution points and a central hub north of London designed to handle over 60 trains a day. Smaller, faster and cheaper trains were also used. For a while, this brought the traffic back but the switch to road continued, with the mail trains and the Travelling Post Offices ceasing to run in 2004. In the 19th century railways all over the world followed the British model.

The speeding mail train is about to collect the leather mail sacks from the trackside apparatus.

Lunch is served in the elegant setting of a Pullman restaurant car, perhaps on a popular holiday route in the late 1930s.

The Dining Car

Until the late 1870s passengers travelling on trains had to rely on station buffets for supplies of food and drink but this all changed with the introduction of the first Pullman car with at seat service in 1879.

From then on, dining or restaurant cars, with their own kitchen cars, became a popular feature on many main line services. Pullmans, either individual carriages attached to express trains or complete sets, were operated independently of the railway companies and passengers paid a supplement to use them.

Initially they were only available to first class passengers, but this changed as dining on the train became a popular habit, with conventional restaurant and buffet cars widely used on expresses all over Britain.

Dining cars were at their peak in the 1930s but were popular until the end of British Rail in the 1990s.

Pullman car Phyllis in typical livery, built for the LNER's Queen of Scots express.

A pioneering diesel electric locomotive, designed by the LMS but built for British Railways, sets off on a night journey.

The Night Train

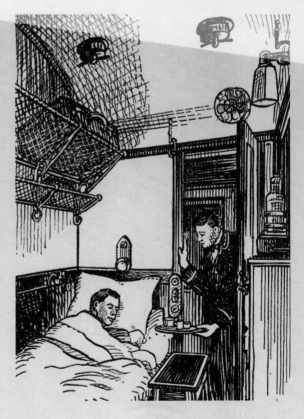

From the early days, trains were operated at night, despite the difficulties imposed by primitive signalling and limited visibility, and round the clock operating soon became the norm, particularly for goods trains, mail and newspaper trains and trains carrying food supplies such as milk and fish.

Track maintenance has also always been an important nocturnal activity. The sight and sound of a train racing through the night soon became a familiar and often dramatic experience all over the network, especially for those living near main lines.

From the 1880s sleeping cars were gradually introduced, initially for Pullman services or first class passengers only but soon becoming universally available as an ever-expanding network of sleeper services spread across the railway map. At first, sleeping and day compartments could be interchangeable, but soon the dedicated sleeper car became dominant, complete with proper beds, toilet and refreshment facilities and a permanent attendant.

Despite being built by many independent companies for their own uses, sleeping cars quickly developed a familiar pattern in their design and layout, leading to the standardised vehicles common throughout the network through the 20th century.

Night traffic was greatly increased during war time, reflecting both much heavier use and the needs of security. Although greatly diminished, some sleeper services are still operating and so the night train lives on, along with the busy overnight freight services.

Night.

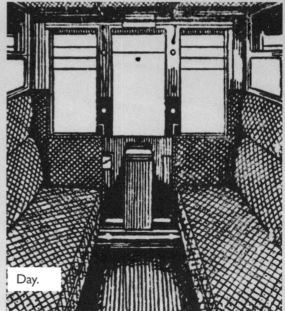

Day.

A late-night express races along the embankment beside the sea in South Devon.

With the firelight from the cab reflected on the smoke streaming from the locomotive, this picture captures the drama of a night express racing past the signals, a familiar sight on Britain's main lines in the 1950s.

After a Royal visit to Swindon works, Princess Elizabeth travels on the footplate of the GWR locomotive Princess Elizabeth.

Royal Trains

Queen Victoria was the first British monarch to travel by train, on 13 June 1842. This opened a new era for Royal travel and a number of Royal carriages and trains were built by various railway companies from the early 1840s onwards.

Lavishly equipped and self-contained, they generally included day and night compartments, the former with office facilities and the latter with bathrooms, for the King and Queen and other members of the Royal family, full catering facilities, and living and sleeping accommodation for staff.

The planning and operation of Royal journeys was very complicated, particularly as Queen Victoria would not allow the train to travel at more than 40 miles per hour.

In addition, in the early days no trains were permitted to pass the Royal train in the opposite direction, except mail trains. Nevertheless, Queen Victoria was a frequent traveller, using the various Royal trains available to her for Royal visits, to show herself to her people, and for journeys to Osborne House, Balmoral and, later, Sandringham.

King Edward VII allowed much faster speeds, and new Royal trains were built for him and Queen Alexandra in 1903 by the London & North Western and London, Brighton & South Coast Railways.

Royal trains were used extensively through the 20th century, and had important roles during both World Wars as they allowed

The Royal train is equipped with full catering and dining facilities, for both formal and informal occasions.

Above: The lounge and a bedroom on the Royal train used for the King and Queen's tour of South Africa in 1947.
Below: Princess Elizabeth's bedroom on the Royal train.

The Queen's day compartment on the Royal train built for King Edward VII and Queen Alexandra in 1903 by the LNWR.

George V and George VI to travel around the country in secret and with great security as the train could be stabled at night in remote sidings. Today, there is still a Royal train, a handsome set of carriages rebuilt to modern standards by British Rail in 1985, but it is used only a few times a year by the Queen or other members of the Royal family.

Parcels traffic was an important part of the railway's freight business, with many scheduled services linking major stations.

GOODS TRAINS

The earliest railways were built for the transport of coal and other mineral traffic, usually from mines and quarries to local harbours.

This pattern was to remain unchanged well into the steam era and it was not until the 1830s that the issue of carrying passengers was properly addressed. Even then, goods remained the primary concern of most railway companies, mainly because freight revenues generally exceeded the income from passenger traffic throughout the 19th century and into the 20th century. The goods train was, therefore, always a familiar sight on Britain's railways and even the smallest stations usually had a goods yard.

Initially, the railways concentrated on bulk cargoes such as coal, which remained the mainstay of the network for decades to support both a coal-fired country and a thriving export business. However, as the network spread across Britain, so the transport of goods rapidly diversified, until the railways became the vital carrier of everything the nation needed or produced, from the major factory to the village shop.

For this to operate smoothly, there had to be a precisely controlled documentation and distribution system, to track the nature and whereabouts of every goods wagon and its load.

This was based on the nationwide network of goods yards and the big marshalling yards where wagons were exchanged between the various railway companies and then assembled into the relevant trains.

By this means, a wagon load of coal or a spare part for a threshing machine could be successfully transported by rail across the country.

In goods yards big and small the sorting of wagons was done by shunting, a largely manual process except in the mechanised marshalling yards.

Goods yards in large towns and cities were massive, to handle all kinds of supplies and goods traffic coming in and out.

Shunting locomotives were generally used to move the actual wagons around but some smaller yards relied on horses.

The core of the system was the mixed goods train, running to regular schedules and connecting all parts of the country.

In addition, there were many special goods services, carrying dedicated cargoes such as milk, fish, fruit and vegetables and other foodstuffs such as grain and flour, oil and petrol, chemicals, a variety of livestock from pigeons to cattle and race horses, cement and a great range of minerals, along with parcels and newspapers.

The heart of the railway freight operation is the marshalling yard where goods wagons are exchanged and trains are assembled.

Another important part of regular railway business was the overnight distribution of newspapers on scheduled services.

There were also special services for the military, and wagons designed for unusual cargoes such as engineering and electrical components.

From the 1930s the process began to be simplified by the use of containers, and now container trains dominate modern international railway freight systems.

With coal the railway's major cargo, this scene of an LNER freight locomotive heading a long coal train was commonplace.

The checking of tickets was traditionally one of the many duties of the guard on a passenger train.

GUARDS

Although they took their name from the armed guards that travelled on mail coaches, railway guards quickly developed their distinctive and responsible role.

Initially they were brakesmen, for carriages and wagons had separate braking systems, and that primary task remained important on goods trains, where the guard travelled in a special brakevan, or guard's van, at the end of the train.

The guard was in charge of the train, and on passenger trains this put him in a very responsible but highly respected position.

Duties included despatching the train from the station, time and record keeping, the care of passengers, luggage, parcels, animals and children travelling on their own, and the inspection of tickets.

With driver and fireman hard at work, a King Class locomotive
is made ready for its day's duties in a Western Region shed.

IN THE SHEDS

A steam locomotive enjoys fundamental constructional and operational details little changed since the early days. However, as working machines they do require constant attention and maintenance and this is complicated by the fact that each one seems to have its own characteristics. Preparing a locomotive for a day's work includes thorough cleaning and polishing, extensive oiling and lubrication, carrying out a range of mechanical checks and adjustments, filling the water tanks and the coal bunkers, and setting and lighting the fire.

The classic type of locomotive shed is the roundhouse, with lines radiating out from a central turntable.

Shed duties include the thorough cleaning and daily maintenance and oiling of locomotives before they go out on duty.

With the fire burning and steam pressure rising, a locomotive is made ready in a Southern Region shed.

Large sheds are equipped with automatic coal hoists, with elevators for the coal wagons and shutes to load the coal directly into the locomotive's tender.

Other duties have to be carried out at the end of the day's work, before the locomotive can be 'put to bed.'

With hundreds of steam engines all over the country needing this daily attention, the answer was to build a network of sheds where locomotives could be housed when not in use, coaled and watered and maintained as necessary. These ranged from small sheds designed for one or two locomotives, and usually located at the ends of branch lines, to huge ones serving major stations and city termini.

Busy freight lines also required big sheds, for example in the coal fields of South Wales. There are several types of shed.

The classic, and one of the earliest, is the roundhouse, with a central turntable and tracks radiating out in a circle, on which the locomotives are housed facing inwards. Vents above the tracks carry smoke and steam up through the roof. Semi-circular versions were also made.

More common is a long linear shed, in brick, stone or other materials, including concrete, with several parallel tracks for the locomotives. Some were built as through sheds, with access from both ends.

At the other end of the scale, the small country and branch line sheds were often little more than a garage, with doors at one end.

A typical scene at the start of the day in a busy main line shed.

Steam locomotives consume huge amounts of water, so sheds and stations are equipped with water towers. The turntable is also a vital part of any large shed.

All had to have facilities for handling coal and water, along with large quantities of ash, and the larger ones were often equipped with workshops and machinery for repairs and heavy maintenance, for example lathes, cranes and wheel drops. Staff rooms, offices and catering facilities were usually included.

Turntables were commonplace in the larger sheds, but were rare on branch lines which were often operated by railcars or 'push-pull' sets designed to be driven from either end.

Sheds were often surrounded by extensive sidings, for coal and oil trucks, other goods wagons and locomotives awaiting repair or out of use.

There were hundreds of sheds all over Britain, some of which dated back to the early years of the railways.

Where a town was served by stations belonging to more than one railway company, each would have its own shed, resulting in considerable duplication. There were also sheds dedicated to the maintenance of carriages and freight wagons. The shed network was rationalised during the 1920s and 1930s and under British Railways each shed was given an identifying code, usually a letter and a number. A cast-iron plate, bearing the code, would be attached to every locomotive's smokebox door to show the shed or depot where it was based.

Carriages require regular cleaning and maintenance which is often carried out in the carriage sheds or sidings.

The shed was an integral part of the railways throughout the steam age and always popular with railway enthusiasts keen to see large collections of locomotives, but it became increasingly redundant as steam locomotives were withdrawn.

Some sheds were closed and quickly demolished, and some were simply abandoned and left to decay until the land on which they stood was required for redevelopment. A few, deemed to be of architectural or historical interest, have been listed and preserved.

Others lived on to house a new generation of diesel and electric locomotives though this was usually a temporary expedient as modern railway vehicles are maintained and stored in different ways.

The steam shed is, therefore, on the list of once familiar railway structures now likely to become extremely rare, if not actually extinct.

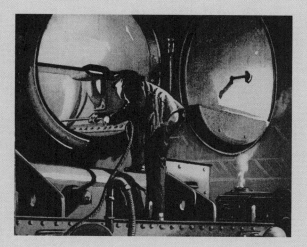

A main line terminus in the middle of the day is always busy and full of varied and interesting activity.

At the STATION

The station is the most enduring and universally familiar part of railway life, yet there was no such thing until the 1830s.

The first railway companies had to develop the station from scratch, without any obvious architectural, functional or social precedents, though as a building it incorporated elements of the coaching inn, the port, the market place, the castle and even the church. Early stations often took their architectural form from domestic or historical architecture, but a distinct building type quickly emerged that reflected the functional needs of the railway. These included the safe running of trains and their maintenance, the management of passengers and their luggage within a public space, the sale of tickets, waiting and refreshment rooms and other facilities, the supply of a variety of staff with specific duties and the ability to operate around the clock and maintain a strict timetable.

Platform One at London's
Paddington station is the departure
point for many of the Great Western's
most famous expresses.

The form and style of the main line railway station or terminus was established by the 1840s, though there were many variations in terms of functional layout or architectural detail. At the same time, the small country or village station was also developed, with more limited facilities and clearer links to contemporary or vernacular domestic architecture.

In its most basic form, the rural station could be just a platform with some kind of rudimentary shelter for waiting passengers, though most small stations had some kind of staffing.

This country station, on the Southern Region's electric network, still has a busy goods yard for coal and other supplies.

Milk churns, luggage, a school trunk and vending machines are all part of station life.

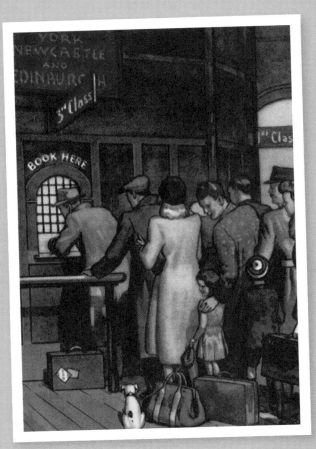

Passengers queue patiently at the ticket office.

In the early days, the management of the railways was based on military lines, and so there was a clear hierarchy for the station staff, often reflected by the types of uniform. At the head was the station master, a figure of great authority and responsibility, and beneath him the equivalent of officers, NCOs and other ranks, all with well-defined duties that ensured the smooth running of the station. These Victorian traditions have been altered by time but the railway station is still a centre of commercial and social activity, usually at the heart of a town or city, and therefore distinct from any other public location dedicated to transport such as an airport.

Apart from the railway-related activities such as the selling of tickets and the giving out of information, large stations often have shops, hotels, restaurants, bars, other catering outlets and connections with buses and taxis.

Large main line stations are continuously busy with a mixture of long-distance and local services.

In the past the list was much longer, and sometimes included luggage and package handling, telegraph offices, post offices and even cinemas.

Staffing levels fell steadily through the second half of the 20th century and now many quite large stations have limited staffing and few facilities, while many rural ones are unmanned. What has not been lost, however, is the excitement and turmoil of activity associated with the arrival and departure of trains, something that has always been present in any station since the start of the railways.

Many stations have kiosks selling sweets and cigarettes.

Also important is the legacy of great architecture created by railway companies, past and present. Styles may vary, but the functional needs of a station have determined a very distinct type of building whose scale, grandeur and sense of detail are reflective of the ambitions of the railways that built them.

A Southern Railway Schools class locomotive takes a West
Country express out of London's Waterloo station.

With a few final waves from the platform, the guard gives the 'right away' and the express is ready to depart.

A signal box on the London Midland Region. The locomotive Royal Scots Fusilier can be seen passing the box at the head of a passenger train.

SIGNALS & SIGNALLING

In the early days traffic control on railways was rudimentary and trains were directed by men with flags, or other visual signalling devices. Operating difficulties and frequent accidents brought about steady improvements, with communications made easier by the electric telegraph from the 1840s.

The first major change was the gradual introduction from the 1850s of the interlocking systems between signals and points, to avoid train drivers being given incomplete or conflicting information. Next came the block system which used the telegraph to manage the movement of trains by dividing the line into sections, or blocks, all controlled individually. Through the 19th century this gradually became more sophisticated and is still the basis for signalling today. The operation of the block system also increased greatly the importance of the signalman, and so signal boxes, fully equipped for continual use, became a familiar part of the lineside on every railway route in Britain.

79

This modern all-electric signal box controls a big city terminal station.

Many of the traditional manually operated lever-controlled signal boxes are still in use, but they are slowly being replaced.

The life of a signalman was demanding, for he would spend long hours in the box, sometimes alone and often at night, particularly on country lines, with the responsibility for controlling and logging all train movements in the section covered by his box. At large stations the signal box was usually part of the infrastructure or on the platform, but many were in remote country areas, often a long way from other people or buildings. The burden of responsibility and decision-making weighed heavily on signalmen, with the result that their actions or mistakes sometimes caused accidents, particularly in the early days. Nowadays most major boxes are electrically operated, but the old image of the signalman controlling his section by manually operating a set of heavy levers has not entirely disappeared. In the 20th century the emphasis has been on

TRACK SIGNALS

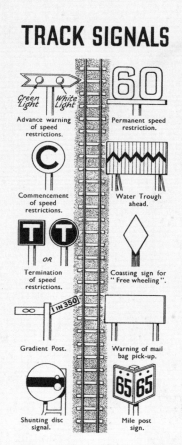

standardisation and the application of new technology, such as radio and electronic control, with the latter ultimately making the signal box redundant. The traditional metal or wood semaphore signals, which date back in one form or another to the dawn of railways and which singly or in groups on gantries were such a major feature in the railway landscape, are also disappearing as the network is increasingly controlled by standard electric coloured light signals.

Coloured light signals, offering greater visibility and safety, have replaced the old semaphore ones on main lines.

VIADUCTS

One of the greatest challenges faced by early railway engineers was the design and construction of large viaducts, often on a scale hitherto unknown for such structures. Remarkable examples were being built as early as 1830.

Many followed the familiar pattern of a long sequence of supporting arches in brick or stone, using techniques first developed by the Romans, but from the start engineers were adventurous.

Robert Stephenson, the son of the inventor of The Rocket, invented the long wrought iron box or tube, while Brunel developed the suspension bridge in ways that were generally thought impossible.

Many materials were used during the 19th century, including timber and concrete, though most common were brick, stone and wrought iron, or combinations of those materials, the shortcomings of cast iron having quickly been established.

With men hard at work on the endless task of painting the Forth Bridge, an express makes its way through the complicated mass of steel girders high above the Forth that make this bridge one of the engineering wonders of the world.

By the end of the 19th century, structural steel was in use, having been pioneered on a grand scale by the Forth Bridge, whose cantilever structure is still one of the engineering wonders of the world.

There were some disasters, notably the collapse of Sir Thomas Bouch's first Tay Bridge, but more remarkable was the largely successful way so many engineers rose to the challenge of pushing forward the boundaries of knowledge.

Viaducts came in all forms and sizes, with some featuring an American-style girder structure supported on thin iron piers, and some used triangulated trusses. Others were built to swing or elevate to allow the passage of shipping.

Primarily functional structures, viaducts have nonetheless a natural elegance, with an instinctive sense of balance and style so typical of the railway age.

A Western Region express slowly crosses Brunel's Royal Albert
bridge, suspended high above the Tamar.

With Newcastle in the background, a long London-bound express curves away from the King Edward VII bridge.

R.O.WAY

An LNER A3 locomotive, in British Railways blue livery, hauls the up Aberdonian across the Tay bridge, with the piers from the old bridge still visible alongside.

Some engineers allowed an element of decoration and ornament, sometimes to echo adjacent buildings of much greater age. Gothic details and battlements are, therefore, not uncommon. The scale is remarkable, with many over a hundred feet high and some up to a mile in length, with the track carried on more than twenty arches. There are hundreds all over Britain, with many Victorian structures in daily use. Others are still standing on lines closed long ago, used sometimes as footpaths or cycle tracks. All are enduring memorials to the skills of Victorian railway engineers.

A typical scaled-down LNER Pacific is ready to depart on the 15 inch gauge Romney, Hythe & Dymchurch Railway.

Narrow Gauge & Miniature Railways

Narrow gauge railways were built all over Britain for a number of reasons, including reduced construction and operating costs, difficult or demanding terrain and the nature of the traffic.

The majority were essentially local enterprises, primarily designed for the carriage of minerals such as slate from quarries to local harbours or main line railways. The gauges used varied extensively throughout the country and the locomotives and rolling stock used were built either by the railways themselves or by specialist manufacturers.

In the latter part of the 19th century passenger carrying became gradually more important, particularly as the mineral traffic declined and tourism became popular, particularly in Wales.

Following the passing of the Light Railway Act in the 1890s, some lines were built specifically for passenger and tourist traffic, usually serving areas of scenic beauty.

Generally individual and sometimes eccentric, narrow gauge railways retained their popularity until the 1930s, when improved road transport, especially motor coaches, seriously reduced their appeal.

Many were closed, but some were revived from the 1950s and have developed new lives as heritage lines. Some industrial lines enjoyed a long life, notably those serving the

One of Britain's earliest, most distinctive and still surviving narrow gauge lines is the Ffestiniog Railway in North Wales.

gas, chemical and paper-making industries, and a range of specialist quarries, along with a number of military railways.

Miniature railways, by definition with a track gauge, or width, of 15 inches or less, came into prominence as passenger-carrying lines from the early years of the 20th century, when a number of longer routes, such as the Romney, Hythe and Dymchurch Light Railway, were developed for tourist use. At the same time, the miniature railway became an essential part of many seaside and holiday resorts, with large numbers opening all over Britain. Many are still operating today. Locomotives are usually scaled-down replicas of main line engines, built by amateur engineers or specialist makers.

Smaller gauges, usually between about 7 inches and under 3 inches, have generally been associated with model and toy railways.

England's other famous 15 inch gauge miniature line is the Ravenglass & Eskdale Railway in Cumbria.

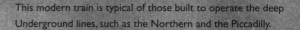
This modern train is typical of those built to operate the deep Underground lines, such as the Northern and the Piccadilly.

IN THE UNDERGROUND

The world's first passenger-carrying underground railway was opened in 1863, linking Paddington with Farringdon Road. It was constructed by the 'cut and cover' system and so followed closely the streets on the surface.

The first trains were steam-hauled, and steam was to remain the main source of power until the 1890s, when electricity began to take over. This pioneering line proved to be popular and so the network quickly expanded, with new routes being added in the 1860s by the Metropolitan, District and Hammersmith Railways. By the 1890s this primarily 'cut and cover' network served many parts of central London and some of the closer suburbs.

In 1890 the world's first deep level, or 'tube', railway was opened. This was the City and South London line, connecting King William Street in the City to Stockwell, south of the Thames.

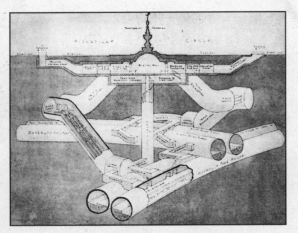
A drawing of Piccadilly Circus station reveals its complexity.

The route was cut by tunnelling shields, a technique first developed by Brunel for the Thames Tunnel. The trains were powered by electricity and stations were equipped with hydraulic lifts. This short line set the pattern for the future and other deep electric-powered 'tube' lines soon followed, including railways that were the basis of what were to become familiar as the Central, Piccadilly, Northern, Bakerloo and Waterloo & City lines.

All the early underground railways were built by independent companies, some of which were supported by main line companies such as the Great Western.

Banks of escalators, seen here at Tottenham Court Road station, underline the Underground's modern image.

Modern, streamlined trains were introduced on some
Underground routes in the 1930s.

Outside central London, many Underground lines run on the surface to connect with outlying and suburban areas.

In 1902 a number of the independents came together to form a new company called Underground Electric Railways. Backed by American finance, this organisation modernised the electric power supply system and the signalling and added electric lifts and elevators. It also developed a uniform corporate look for trains, stations and signage, and made universal the Underground name for the whole network. Some lines remained independent but they were all brought together in 1933 with the formation of the London Passenger Transport Board, which brought together buses, trams and the Underground under the London Transport heading. Modernisation and expansion followed, including the building of new lines, along with the continuation of the famous modern image publicity that had made London Transport famous all over the world. The Victorian network has since been expanded by both Underground and overground lines to join central London to most of the outer suburbs. Early underground lines were also built in Glasgow and Liverpool, and the systems developed in Britain were copied by many other countries.

The Metropolitan Railway had a fleet of electric locomotives to operate the longest routes in the Underground network.

The Hook Continental boat train en route from London Liverpool Street to Harwich, to connect with the ferry for Holland.

GOING ABROAD

Railway companies in Britain began to operate their own cross-Channel services from the early 1850s and by the 1860s many routes had been opened. Many were based on south coast harbours such as Folkestone, Dover, Newhaven, Southampton and Weymouth, which were often also under railway control. Competition between railway companies meant there were many routes to France and Belgium.

At London's Charing Cross station the South Eastern & Chatham Railway's Paris boat train is about to depart.

The sleeping cars for the Night Ferry, the direct service linking London and Paris, are shunted onto the train ferry at Dover.

However, also important were services across the Irish Sea from English, Welsh and Scottish ports, and across the North Sea to Holland and the Baltic from east coast ports. Many ports and harbours were extensively developed by railway companies and some, such as Harwich Parkeston Quay, were created from scratch for international services.

In all, over fifty railway-owned shipping companies ran services out of Britain at various times and over 1000 ships were involved, including ferries, pleasure steamers, cargo vessels, tugs and other types. Later ferries were also able to carry cars and commercial vehicles, traffic that was to become dominant from the 1960s. With the ferries came special boat trains, running from main line termini all over Britain, many of which became well known for their Pullman or luxury services.

Most famous of all was the Golden Arrow, a high-speed train linking London and Paris in a little over six hours, including the Channel crossing on a dedicated ferry. Two trains were involved, a Pullman between London and Dover, and a Wagons-Lits service between Calais and Paris.

The only passenger train that actually crossed the Channel on a ship was the Night Ferry sleeping car service linking London to Paris and Brussels. Apart from this service, train ferries, the first of which was built in 1850 to carry wagons across the Firth of Forth, were freight-only vessels and several routes operated to transport freight wagons across the Channel and the North Sea until the opening of the Channel tunnel.

The LNER's train ferry leaves Harwich for Zeebrugge.

Kangaroos leap away from the track as an express speeds across the Australian plains.

TRAINS OF THE EMPIRE

The rapid growth of the British Empire during the 19th century opened up new markets to a great variety of manufacturers and traders in Britain. At the same time, railways were important for the successful economic, social and political development of the Empire and so British engineers and construction and manufacturing companies were heavily involved in creating most of the railway networks in the parts of the world that were under British control. Particularly important were India, Canada, Australia, New Zealand, South Africa and other parts of the African continent.

The Victoria terminus of the Great Indian Peninsular Railway in Bombay, a magnificent station with echoes of St Pancras.

A streamlined 4-8-2 locomotive built in Britain for the
demanding terrain on New Zealand Railways' express routes.

A streamlined Pacific locomotive at the head of New South Wales Railways' Sydney to Newcastle express.

A Canadian Pacific Railway transcontinental express climbs through the Rockies on its route across Canada.

An express winds its way through the Canadian Rockies.

India's first railway was opened in 1853, near Bombay, and this inspired the rapid development of railways across the country.

By 1880 there were 9,000 miles in operation, and by 1929, this had reached 41,000 miles, a massive network that is still the backbone of the nation's transport system.

The railway came earlier to Canada with the opening in 1836 of the line linking the St Lawrence with Lake Champlain, on which Charles Dickens was a famous early traveller. The line's first locomotive, Dorchester, was built in Newcastle.

Other railways followed but the main event was the completion in 1885 of the first transcontinental route by the Canadian Pacific Railway. Australia's first railway was a mining line near Newcastle, opened in 1831, but it was not until 1854 that the nation's first passenger-carrying railway was completed, from Melbourne to Port Melbourne.

Other pioneering lines opened in New South Wales in 1855 and South Australia a year later and from these a busy network quickly developed, though the use of different gauges from state to state was a limitation for a long time. The first line in New Zealand came in 1863, from Christchurch to Ferrymead.

Africa represented a greater challenge to the railway builders as a number of nations were

A powerful 4-8-2 locomotive heads South African Railway's
Union Express between Johannesburg and Capetown.

involved, all with colonial ambitions and all keen to support their own local railway industries. The continent's first railway was actually in Egypt, completed in 1856 to link Alexandria and Cairo.

However, the most important area of British interest was South Africa, whose railway map was started in 1860. Subsequent development was by a number of independent companies but, following the Act of Union in 1910, they were all merged together as South African Railways in 1916.

In British East Africa the major event was the opening in 1901 of the long Uganda Railway, destined to become a major freight route inland from the sea. However, the major railway dream of late 19th-century politicians and industrialists in several competing colonial powers was the Cape to Cairo line, destined never to be built.

A modern electric locomotive hauls an Indian
Peninsular Railway express out of Bombay station.

GIP

No 4002

D·B·WAY

The Khedive's personal train, on the Egyptian Government Railways, was built in Britain in 1862.

The famous spiral on the narrow-gauge Darjeeling Railway in Northern India, which climbs to over 7,000 feet.

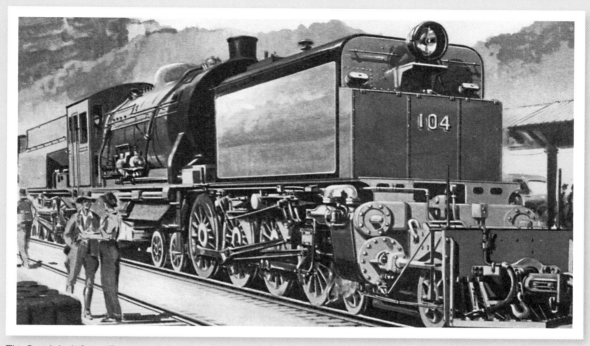

This British-built Beyer-Garratt articulated locomotive is ready for work on the Kenya section of East African Railways.

Double heading is common on many railways of the Empire. This is the Trans-Canada Limited.

RAILWAYS AT WAR

The strategic importance of railways became apparent during various 19th-century campaigns in various parts of the world, notably the Crimean War, the American Civil War, the Franco-Prussian War and the South African War.

In Britain, there was a government requirement from 1842 that the railways would move troops as needed and by the 1870s the government was empowered to take control of the railway network while working closely with the railway companies.

For a while the emphasis was on the transport of troops and equipment to and from the south coast embarkation ports but a number of dedicated military railways were built, often to connect training areas, barracks and depots.

In wartime, many main line services operated as usual, with junctions and important installations guarded by the army.

Blackouts and restrictions, and a proliferation of uniforms, changed the look of major termini, such as London's Waterloo.

In a massive operation that involved hundreds of special trains, children were evacuated out of London in 1940.

Despite the threat from air raids, the railways, upon which the nation and the war effort depended, had to carry on.

Marshalling yards and freight services were often the target during the Blitz in 1940, and throughout the war.

From the 1860s, plans to prepare the railways for the outbreak of war were regularly drawn up and revised but the government did not exercise its control option until the start of World War I in 1914 and the establishment of a Railway Executive Committee.

Throughout this conflict the railways were heavily engaged, moving troops, equipment and supplies, expanding the ports and their rail connections, setting up train ferry routes and keeping moving essential supplies such as coal.

In addition, there were ambulance trains, all on top of the ordinary civilian passenger and freight services which continued to operate, though on reduced timetables. Several hundred locomotives were taken for use in battle areas overseas, and nearly half the railway work force of military age joined the services, allowing women to replace them in many areas of railway operations.

Railway workshops were turned over to the production of ammunition and military equipment. Despite this, the railways rose to the challenge and services were maintained.

In World War II the government again took control of the railways but the burden through this conflict was much heavier.

Apart from the movement of troops and equipment, and the maintenance of domestic passenger and freight services, the railways were responsible for the evacuation of women and children from London and other cities. There was the added danger of aerial bombing, prompting the use of blackouts for trains and stations and, in the early years of the war, the risk of gas attacks or chemical warfare had to be taken seriously.

To counter the threat of invasion, armoured trains were brought into service along the south coast and in Scotland.

Once again, many railway workers were called up for military service, with women taking many of their jobs and once again some railway workshops were switched to the production of armaments, notably tanks. The evacuation from Dunkirk threw a massive burden onto the railways but the network coped, as it did again when Canadian and American soldiers began to arrive in Britain in huge numbers, despite the constant disruption caused by bombing raids.

Preparing the army for its departure for the North African campaigns required 440 troop trains and 1,150 freight trains.

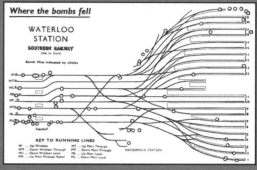

Where the bombs fell

WATERLOO
STATION
SOUTHERN RAILWAY
(Not to Scale)

Bomb Hits indicated by circles

KEY TO RUNNING LINES

W ... Up Windsor		MT ... Up Main Through
WT ... Down Windsor Through		MT ... Down Main Through
WL ... Down Windsor Local		ML ... Up Main Local
MR ... Up Main Through Relief		ML ... Down Main Local

NECROPOLIS STATION

When the war spread to North Africa, the Middle East, the Mediterranean and other overseas theatres, the railways played a crucial role in the build-up to these campaigns. However, the finest hour of the railway network was its role in the preparations and continued support for D-Day and the Normandy campaign.

Britain's railways can claim to have been a great success during World War II, despite all the dangers and operating difficulties, underlining the famous statement made by the German General Ludendorff in 1918, that in war locomotives can sometimes be more important than guns. By the end of the war, the railway network was in a poor state, the result of years of overuse and inadequate maintenance and investment, and of damage and destruction by enemy action, a situation that lead directly to the network's nationalisation as British Railways.

With government support, the railways were then able to develop plans for a new future, with rebuilt routes, new and restored stations, new locomotives and rolling stock and a modernisation plan designed to make Britain's railway network one of the best in the world.

Fast freight services, including the delivery of tanks and other war material from the factories, were essential for the war effort.

Many Underground stations were turned into safe shelters for thousands of Londoners during the Blitz.

With the end of the war, stations all over Britain witnessed many happy scenes as service men and women returned home.

ACCIDENTS

When the Liverpool & Manchester Railway was opened in 1830, the day was marred by the death of William Huskisson MP, in what is generally regarded as Britain's first serious railway accident. Since then, accidents have been a feature of railway life, with the usual causes being inadequate signalling, poor maintenance of track and trains, and human error.

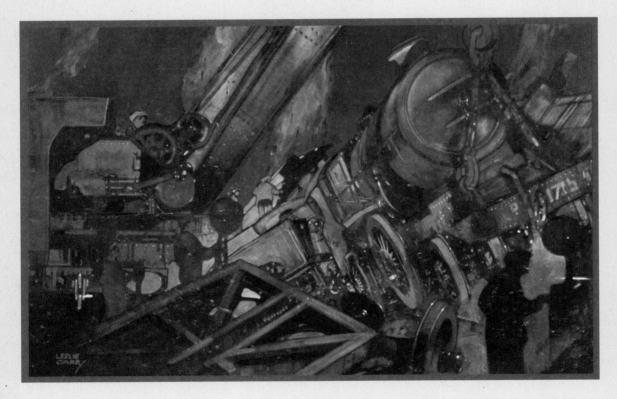

The effects of a derailment or collision at high speed are often horrendous, resulting in widespread destruction, loss of life and many injuries.

This dramatic illustration shows the collapse of the Tay Bridge during a storm in December 1879, when seventy-five people lost their lives. A poor design by the engineer, Sir Thomas Bouch, caused Britain's worst bridge disaster.

PICTURE AND ARTIST CREDITS

Images used in this book have come from many sources. Many such images inevitably remain anonymous, despite attempts at tracing or identifying their origin. If photographs or images have been used without due credit or acknowledgement, through no fault of our own, apologies are offered. If you believe this is the case, please let us know because we would like to give full credit in any future edition.

Chapter One EARLY RAILWAYS
p8 *Exide Batteries*, annual calendar 1960s, artist credit C & W Meadway

Chapter Two GREAT LOCOMOTIVES
p12 *Off By Train ABC*, Raphael Tuck, artist unknown; p13 *The Railway Album*, Sampson, Low, Marston & Co, artist Jobson; p14 *The Railway Album*, Sampson, Low, Marston & Co, artist unknown; p15 *My New Train Book*, Nelson, artist unknown; p15 *The Book of Railways*, Birn Brothers, artist R M Clark; p15 *Trains*, Nelson, artist unknown; p16 *The Railway Album*, Sampson, Low, Marston & Co, artist Jobson; p17 *The Railway Album*, Sampson, Low, Marston & Co, artist Jobson

Chapter Three HOW IT WORKS
p18 *The Railway Album*, Sampson, Low, Marston & Co, artist unknown; p19 *The Railway Album*, Sampson, Low, Marston & Co, artist unknown; p20 *Railways Today*, Frederick Warne, 1929, artist unknown; p20 *Railways Today*, Frederick Warne, 1929; p21 *The Railway Album*, Sampson, Low, Marston & Co; p21 *The Railway Album*, Sampson, Low, Marston & Co

Chapter Four BUILDING TRAINS
p22 *Railway Pictures*, Nelson, artist Leslie Carr; p25 *The Book of Railways*, Birn Brothers, artist unknown

Chapter Five ON THE FOOTPLATE
pp26–27 *Off by Train ABC*, Raphael Tuck, artist unknown

Chapter Six TRAINS WITH NAMES
p28 *The Book of Railways*, Birn Brothers, artist unknown; p30 (TL) *Trains*, Nelson, artist R B Way; p30 (TR) Postcard, artist G P Micklewright ; p31 (T) *The Book of Railways*, Birn Brothers, artist R M Clark; p30 (B) *The Book of Railways*, Birn Brothers, artist R M Clark; p32 *The Book of Railways*, Birn Brothers, artist R M Clark; p32 *The Book of Railways*, Birn Brothers, artist R M Clark; p33 *The Book of Railways*, Birn Brothers, artist R M Clark; p34 (T) *The Wonder Book of Railways*, Ward Lock, artist F W Moore; p34 (B) *My travel Book by Land and Sea*, Frederick Warne, artist F W Moore; p35 *Trains*, Nelson, artist R B Way; p36 (T) *My New Train Book*, Nelson, artist unknown; p36 (B) Postcard, artist Alan Anderson; p37 *Timothey's Book of Trains*, Collins, artist T E North

Chapter Seven THE MAIL TRAIN
p38 *All Change Here*, Humphrey Milford Oxford University Press, 1938, artist Geoffrey Eyles; p41 (B) 'The Night Mail', LMS poster, 1924, artwork by Sir William Orpen; p43 *The Book of Railways*, Birn Brothers, artist unknown

Chapter Eight THE DINING CAR
p44 *Off By Train ABC*, Raphael Tuck, artist unknown; p45 *Railways of Today*, Frederick Warne, 1929, artist unknown

Chapter Nine THE NIGHT TRAIN
p46 *The Railway Album*, Sampson, Low, Marston & Co, artist Jobson; p49 *My Book of Trains*, Raphael Tuck, artist unknown

Chapter Ten ROYAL TRAINS
p52–53 All monochrome illustrations from *The Railway Album*, Sampson, Low, Marston. Original sources unknown

Chapter Eleven GOODS TRAINS
p54 *The Book of Railways*, Birn Brothers, artist R M Clark; p56 *Off By Train ABC*, Raphael Tuck, artist unknown; p57 *Timothy's Book of Trains*, Collins, Artist T E North; p58 *Off by Train ABC*, Raphael Tuck, artist unknown; p59 *Railway Pictures*, Nelson, artist Leslie Carr

Chapter Twelve GUARDS
p60 *Off By Train ABC*, Raphael Tuck, artist unknown

Chapter Thirteen IN THE SHEDS
p62 *The Book of Railways*, Birn Brothers, artist R M Clark; p63 *The Railway Album*, Sampson, Low, Marston & Co, artist unknown; p64 *Off By Train ABC*, Raphael Tuck, artist unknown; p64 *The Railway Album*, Sampson, Low, Marston & Co, artist unknown; p64 *My Book of Trains*, Raphael Tuck, artist unknown; p65 *Timothy's Book of Trains*, Collins, artist T E North; p66 *The Book of Railways*, Birn Brothers, artist R M Clark; p67 (L) *Off By Train ABC*, Raphael Tuck, artist unknown; p67 (R) *All About Trains*, 1951, artist Jobson; p68 *Timothy's Book of Trains*, Collins, artist T E North

Chapter Fourteen AT THE STATION
p70 *All Change Here*, Humphrey Milford, Oxford University Press. 1938, artist Geoffrey Eyles; p72 *Railway Pictures*, Nelson, artist Leslie Carr; p73 *My Book of Trains*, Raphael Tuck, artist unknown; p73 *Off By Train ABC*, Raphael Tuck, artist unknown; p75 *Off By Train ABC*, Raphael Tuck, artist unknown; p75 *Timothy's Book of Trains*, Collins, artist T E North; p76 *The Book of Railways*, Birn Brothers, artist R M Clark; p77 *Off By Train ABC*, Raphael Tuck, artist unknown

Chapter Fifteen SIGNALS & SIGNALLING
p78 *All About Trains*, 1951, artist Jobson; P80 *The Book of Railways*, Birn Brothers, artist R M Clark; P81 *Railways of Today*, Frederick Warne, 1929, artist unknown; p82 *Timothy's Book of Trains*, Collins, artist T E North

Chapter Sixteen VIADUCTS
p85 *The Railway Album*, Sampson, Low, Marston & Co, artist unknown; p86 *The Book of Railways*, Birn Brothers, artist R M Clark; p87 *Trains*, Nelson, artist R B Way; p88 *Trains*, Nelson, artist R B Way

ARTIST BIOGRAPHIES

Alan Anderson
No records found.

Leslie Carr 1891–1961
Painter, illustrator, poster designer and commercial artist.
Worked for LNER, SR, LCC Tramways, British Railways, Morris
Motors. Carr was a regular illustrator for *Motor* magazine.

R M Clark
No records found.

Geoffrey Eyles
Son of Charles Eyles, illustrator and comic artist, and brother
of Derek Eyles (1902–1974), noted comic strip and book
illustrator. Worked in the 1930s and 1940s.

Jobson
Possibly Ron Jobson, poster designer, aviation artist and
illustrator for Matchbox Toys and Airfix kits. Working from the
1940s.

Reginald Mayes 1901–1992
Illustrator, poster designer, commercial artist. Worked for
London Transport, later chief staff artist for LMS, designing
posters and leaflets, notably during World War II.

Clifford & Wendy Meadway
Husband and wife design and illustration partnership, famous
for work on the *Look and Learn* book series. Clifford (1921–
1999) specialised in trains and vehicles, and Wendy on wildlife
subjects.

G F Micklewright
No records found.

F Moore
Name used for illustrations issued by the Locomotive
Publishing Company, whose main artist was Thomas Rudd,
working 1890-1930.

Thomas Edward North 1916–1985
Hull-based artist and illustrator, known for childrens' train,
aircraft and car books, also for jigsaw puzzles. Worked during
the late 1930s to 1960s.

Robert Barnard Way 1890–1958
Prolific writer, artist and illustrator, associated with childrens'
books from 1930 to 1958. Also worked for cigarette card
companies.

Norman Wilkinson CBE 1878–1971
Marine painter, illustrator, poster designer, working mainly for
LNER and LMS, inventor of dazzle camouflage in World War II.

ACKNOWLEDGEMENTS

My thanks are due primarily to the railway picture
books I enjoyed as a small boy, the memory of which
was the inspiration for this modern version. The
illustrations, by highly creative but often anonymous,
artists seem even better now than I remember, and
so I am glad to have the chance to celebrate their
achievement. I am particularly grateful to Chrissie,
my wife, whose dedication, enthusiasm and patience,
brought back to life the often damaged illustrations
from the battered and often under-appreciated copies
of the original books that were acquired from antique
and second hand shops, boot fairs and the internet. My
thanks are also due to Verity Muir and the production
team at David & Charles, whose skills helped to make a
real Wonder Book.

INDEX

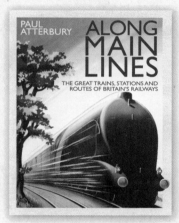
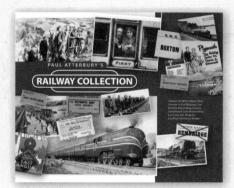

A DAVID & CHARLES BOOK

© F&W Media International, Ltd 2012
David & Charles is an imprint of F&W Media International, Ltd
Brunel House, Forde Close, Newton Abbot, TQ12 4PU, UK

F&W Media International, Ltd is a subsidiary of F+W Media, Inc.,
10151 Carver Road, Cincinnati OH45242, USA

ISBN-13: 978-1-4463-0203-3 Hardback
ISBN-10: 1-4463-0203-2 Hardback

10 9 8 7 6 5 4 3 2 1

Junior Acquisitions Editor: Verity Muir
Art Editor: Anna Fazakerley
Production Manager: Beverley Richardson
Image scanning and presentation: Chrissie Atterbury

Hardback edition printed in China by RR Donnelley for:
F&W Media International, Ltd
Brunel House, Forde Close, Newton Abbot, TQ12 4PU, UK

F+W Media publishes high quality books on a wide range of subjects.
For more great book ideas visit: www.fwmedia.co.uk

SOUTHERN RAILWAY